A Sketchbook of Birds

In a lifetime devoted to his art, Charles Tunnicliffe achieved mastery in several different fields, as an etcher and engraver, water-colourist and book illustrator specialising in natural history subjects. As a bird artist, Tunnicliffe stands supreme as the finest English practitioner since Thomas Bewick.

The present work comprises a selection of pages from Charles Tunnicliffe's many sketchbooks in which he recorded his observations of birds in the field. The earliest sketch included in this book dates from 1934, and the latest from 1962. In all, 123 sketches have been selected from seventeen sketchbooks.

The work is divided into five separate sections: *Seabirds; Waders; Geese, Ducks and Swans; Birds of Prey* and *Miscellaneous Birds*.

A SKETCHBOOK OF BIRDS gives us, as Ian Niall comments in his introduction, a privileged view of the private world of a dedicated artist whose great gifts as a draughtsman were complemented by a countryman's profound understanding of nature and acute observation of birds and animals.

C. F. Tunnicliffe R.A.
A Sketchbook of Birds

Introduction by Ian Niall

VICTOR GOLLANCZ
LONDON

First published in Great Britain in 1979
by Victor Gollancz Ltd

Introduction © Ian Niall 1979
Illustrations © Mrs Dorothy Downes 1979

This edition published in Great Britain in 1999
by Victor Gollancz

An imprint of Orion Books Ltd
Orion House, 5 Upper St Martin's Lane,
London WC2H 9EA

A CIP catalogue record for this book is available
from the British Library

ISBN 0 575 06785 3

Printed and bound in Italy

Contents

Publisher's Note

The sketches reproduced in this book are taken from seventeen sketchbooks filled by the artist between 1934 and 1962. Some of the larger sketches have been slightly reduced in order to fit the page.

Most of the sketches were made at two locations: the island of Anglesey, where Charles Tunnicliffe lived from 1947 until his death in February 1979, and the country near Macclesfield in Cheshire, where he spent the first twenty-odd years of his life, and frequently re-visited.

In nearly all cases, Tunnicliffe noted on his sketches the location and the date of composition; the year of composition and the scientific names of the birds have been added in the captions.

The publisher acknowledges with gratitude the unfailing assistance of the artist's sister, Mrs Dorothy Downes, and of Mr and Mrs Ian Niall, without whom the book could not have been published.

Sadly, Charles Tunnicliffe did not live to see publication of this book, but he saw colour proofs of some of the pictures and took pleasure in discussing and corresponding about publishing details during the planning stages. His last letter, giving details of his early wood-engravings, was received at the Gollancz office on the day of his death.

Introduction
by Ian Niall

In popular imagination a romantic aura surrounds the lives of artists, but I have always believed that any artist who is more than a nine days' wonder must have an essentially practical approach. Great talent is cultivated in interminable days, in years of striving to master a technique, in applying continually a special imagination, which is the artist's gift.

Charles Tunnicliffe, the son of ordinary farming folk from Cheshire, was a man whose application, whose undaunted perseverance, put my own rather superficial approach to most things in shameful shade.

I first knew of him (in common with thousands of others) as the illustrator of Henry Williamson's famous books *Tarka the Otter* (1932) and *Salar the Salmon* (1935). Before this, Tunnicliffe had sold some superb etchings while still a student at the Royal College of Art. Most went into private collections, but some were purchased by the Victoria and Albert Museum in London and the National Gallery, Stockholm. He was quickly making his name as an engraver and illustrator of the first rank, and his work for Williamson was the prelude to a lifetime of illustrating books for authors small and great (Hemingway, Negley Farson, H. E. Bates and Richard Church among them). To all of these, and to many others, Tunnicliffe brought something exceptional, an uncanny sensitivity, the ability to enter the author's fantasy – the mark of the great illustrator.

Twelve or thirteen years ago I met Charles Tunnicliffe for the first time. His home on the island of Anglesey was not far from mine above Llandudno in North Wales. We began to correspond, and to meet from time to time and I formed the idea that I might one day write about his life and art. Although I am neither an ornithologist nor a student of art, I felt that I might bring a certain understanding to the task. We came from similar backgrounds. Eventually I decided to put away other work and prepare a biography. Charles greeted my proposal diffidently (being the most modest of men) but agreed to see me each week. We talked about his early life in Macclesfield, his struggles to make a living as an artist, his marriage, his experiences with the highly inflammable Henry Williamson. Throughout, he would punctuate any reminiscence with amazingly wide ranging observations on birds and animals. For me, our meetings were far more than nostalgia; I was sitting at the feet of a great naturalist and a great observer. Charles had studied birds with an artist's, not a shooting man's, eye. He knew the golden plover's flight, the juvenile plumage of the rare northern variety, the feeding rituals of falcons and cormorants, the precise extent of a snowy owl's wing. This vast knowledge was recorded in his field notes and sketchbooks, an amazing collection of the most detailed study and the finest art in themselves.

As the pages of my notes increased, I felt that it was time to look for a publisher. My friend and fishing companion, David Burnett of Victor Gollancz, needed no second invitation to come up from London and talk about the book with Charles and myself. When he arrived at my house I proceeded to talk him into the ground about *The Life and Art of Charles Tunnicliffe*. On the journey over to Anglesey he kept falling asleep as I continued at length to describe the marvels that Tunnicliffe had shown me, including his drawings for the original wood-engravings for *Tarka*, and his extraordinary 'bird maps', large scale detailed studies of hundreds of birds, some of which I thought might go into my book. On arriving at Shorelands, the house at Malltraeth where Tunnicliffe lived for thirty years, we looked together at the 'bird maps' and then I once again took up with Charles the thread of our previous discussion. My publishing friend had fallen into a kind of reverie over some sketchbooks he had found casually stowed in a cupboard. It seemed to me that he was pondering technical problems. I was afraid that he would say that my book could not be illustrated in the generous way I had hoped. Suddenly he remarked that here was treasure trove. Tunnicliffe's bird sketches were something the world must see. There was nothing like them. They called for the finest possible reproduction, paper and printing. Everyone who loved beautiful work would want to possess a book of the sketches, as a boy wants to keep the exotic butterfly he cups in his hands. Bird-watchers, ornithologists and artists would all be enchanted by it. Tunnicliffe blinked for a moment and smiled at this enthusiasm. In a long life dedicated to his art he had accumulated so much work of such breath-taking quality that he thought no more about it, but we were thinking about it and the need to let the world see it. Would he entrust the priceless sketchbooks to the publisher's care for a while so that the pictures could be photographed? Tunnicliffe had a generous nature and he graciously agreed. And so *A Sketchbook of Birds* was born.

Tunnicliffe's *alter ego* was art. In the face of this unturnable force, his parents accepted that their son must be allowed to cultivate his talent and could not remain to help them on the farm. He went, first by one scholarship to Macclesfield School of Art and then by another to the Royal College of Art. From there he proceeded to exhibit at and then to be admitted to the Royal Academy. In 1977, towards the end of a great career, his name appeared in the Queen's Birthday Honours List. Along the way, and in the course of the busiest lifetime any artist can ever have had, he amassed sketches – some of the best of which are published here. Charles Tunnicliffe's *Sketchbook of Birds* speaks for itself. Writing an introduction to it, I know that my words will be read not before but after the reader has turned the pages in wonder, over and over again.

Tunnicliffe's place in art is assured by virtue of endless work at the easel and drawing board. My problem is to find words to put upon it – obsession, perfectionism, meticulous care, beauty. I remember Charles once quoting me the favourite tag of one of his professors at the Royal Academy one day when we were talking about the nature of art – 'Tell me where is fancy bred, or in the heart or in the head?' There is no answer, but fancy – the conception of beauty – being there, Tunnicliffe fostered it when he could, to the exclusion of everything else, and for a lifetime. People will go on collecting Tunnicliffe's prints, coveting those early etchings – *The Bull, The Cheshire Plain, A Winter Landscape* – coveting also the water-colours snatched up by eager buyers on the first day of the Academy exhibitions, long after most of his contemporaries are forgotten. If I commented further on the *Sketchbook of Birds* it would be to remind those who have seen it that they are enjoying a very privileged view of the quiet life of a private man – and a great artist.

Tan-yr-Allt Cottage
Llandudno, February 1979

Location Notes to the Sketches

The purpose of these brief notes is to enable the reader to locate on a map the sites referred to in Tunnicliffe's sketches. In a few cases, identification of the sites is uncertain. Most sites are either close to Macclesfield, the artist's home town in Cheshire, or on the island of Anglesey, where he made his home in 1947 and where he remained until his death.

Alderley Edge—Cheshire. To the north-west of Macclesfield.

Amlwch—ancient port in north Anglesey.

Anglesey—island situated off the north coast of Wales. First connected to the mainland by Thomas Telford's famous bridge across the Menai Strait.

Beaumaris—Anglesey, at the eastern end of the Menai Strait.

Birtles Pool—west of Macclesfield, in the grounds of Birtles Hall.

Bodorgan headland—south-west Anglesey, north of the Cefni estuary.

Bont Farm—near the artist's home, south-west Anglesey.

Bosley Reservoir—south of Macclesfield, by the A54 and A523 road junction.

Capesthorne Pool—west of Macclesfield in the grounds of Capesthorne Hall.

Cemlyn Lake—on the north coast of Anglesey, west of Amlwch.

Clitheroe—(Bradley Hall) Lancashire.

Clough Brook—a stream near the artist's birthplace, south of Macclesfield.

Cob Lake—by Malltraeth, Anglesey.

Crochan Caffo—a pool in the marshes near Llangaffo, Anglesey.

Dinas Point—by Bodorgan, off the northern shore of the Cefni estuary.

Foel Ferry—near the western end of the Menai Strait on the Anglesey side, opposite Caernarvon (the ferry no longer operates).

Foryd Estuary—North Wales, across the Menai Strait from Anglesey, at the western end.

Gawsworth Pool—south of Macclesfield in the grounds of Gawsworth Hall.

Glan Avon—probably Glanrafon, a farm near the artist's home in Anglesey.

Goldsitch Moss—country area to the south-east of Macclesfield.

Gull Island, Aberdaron—off the coast of north-west Wales. The two islands are usually called 'The Gwyllans'.

Handa Island, Sutherland—Scotland, off the north-west highland coast.

Hawk's-head Clough—near Higher Sutton, Macclesfield.

Iona—island off the south-west shore of Mull, north-west Scotland.

Kendal—south-west Lake District, Westmorland.

Llandwyn lighthouse—Llandwyn Island, south Anglesey, on the southern side of the Cefni estuary.

Lligwy Bay—on the north-east coast of Anglesey.

Llyn Coron—a small lake near Bodorgan railway station, south-west Anglesey.

Macclesfield—Cheshire. The artist's home town, just north of Langley, his birthplace.

Malltraeth Lake—near the artist's home, south-west Anglesey.

Moelfre—on the north-east coast of Anglesey.

Nant Bychan rocks—north-east coast of Anglesey, between Traeth Bychan and Moelfre.

Northwich—Cheshire. A small town to the west of Macclesfield.

Pont Aber Glaslyn—Snowdonia, North Wales, in the mountain pass south of Beddgelert (A498 road).

Porth Aber (usually Porth yr Aber)—near Moelfre on the east coast of Anglesey.

Radnor Mere—a lake south of Nether Alderley, to the north-west of Macclesfield.

Radnor Woods—beech woods south of Nether Alderley, to the north-west of Macclesfield.

Redesmere—a lake west of Macclesfield, Cheshire.

Shorelands—the artist's home by Malltraeth, south-west Anglesey.

South Stack—cliffs off the north-west coast of Holy Island, Anglesey.

Stack Rocks—A group of rocks in St Bride's Bay to the north-east of Skomer Island. In 1938 CFT and his wife were marooned on the island by bad weather for some days and were forced to live off seagull's eggs.

Traeth Bach—estuary in north-west Wales, south of Porthmadog.

Traeth Bychan—a small bay on the north-east coast of Anglesey, south of Moelfre.

Ty Gwyn—south of Cefni Reservoir, Llangefni, Anglesey.

Y Felin—literally 'The Mill', of which there are several near the artist's home on Anglesey. The precise location is unknown.

Seabirds

1 Common gull, *Larus canus*, on the island of Iona, Argyll, September 1934.
2 Great black-backed gull, *Larus marinus*, Iona, September 25th, 1934.
3 Young herring gull, *Larus argentatus*, Iona, September 1934.

Iona Sept. 25th
Gr Black-backed gull.

Seen singly. Sometimes with
a crowd of common gulls resting
on the machair. Today seen
feeding on the body of a dead
dog thrown up at White Sands
bay. Two Hoody crows also feeding
with him.

Seen also in the pastures
behind the farms on rising
ground resting with a young
gull.

In Iona regarded as the king
of thieves and murderers.

From memory.

From life.

2

Young Herring gull.
Iona. Sept.

3

Sept 2nd Moelfre. Immature Herring Gull.
Sat while I drew at a distance of 9 feet.

4

4 Studies of immature herring gull, *Larus argentatus*, Moelfre, September 1944.

Stream running through
shingle beach south of Beaumaris.
Two plumages of Juvenile Black-headed Gull
the sitting bird was pale and browner on scapulars
and wings and had no brown suffusion on sides of
breast and flanks. Amount of colour on heads varies
also

July 13ᵗ

5 Juvenile black-headed gulls, *Larus ridibundus*, near Beaumaris, July 13th, probably 1948.

June 13th. *Our Stack Rocks.*

Scapulars darker grey than wing coverts.
Slight sepia.
Tail pale grey, covert grey whiter tips.
Legs grey & feet.
Beak amber green and yellowish towards the tip. Tube blackish.

Shag and well grown young still in down but with tail and wing quills sprouting. Young often with open beak and its throat throbbing rapidly because of the heat. Here it is lying with its left leg thrust back behind its stumpy tail.

A view from above which accounts for the foreshortening of the adult.

Juvenile scrambling about cliff face. It could fly and later did so. (This drawing from memory)

A more bird with breast paler than back. Scapulars and wing coverts appeared sepia brown with pale wavy-brown edges. Iris appeared pale yellow.

6 Fulmar, *Fulmarus glacialis*, near Stack Rock. June 13th, 1938.
7 Shags, *Phalacrocorax aristotelis:* adult with young, and juvenile. Bodorgan headland, May 1948.

8 Cormorant, *Phalacrocorax carbo*, nestling, Bodorgan headland, July 17th, 1949.
9 Puffins, *Fratercula arctica*, Gull Island, Aberdaron, July 30th, 1935.

Just before landing (1)

(2)

(3)

July 30th. Gull Island, Aberaaron

Puffins still taking fish to their nesting burrows

Lands with feet extended as above
then falls rather clumsily forward on
its breast causing a splash.

Beak actual size
(Probably higher)

Skin round the eye
leaden grey/grey blue

9

June 2nd

Common Terns. Nant Bychan
Rocks.

One preening on a rock. Other
brought a fish to it but preening
bird ignored it and flew away
Other bird at once swallowed fish

10 Common terns, *Sterna hirundo*, one offering a fish. Nant Bychan rocks, June 2nd, 1942.

June 3rd Lligwy Bay.
Pair of little Terns. Suspect they
are the same pair noted at Traeth
Bychan as they were at Lligwy
during high tide when all the sand
at Traeth Bychan is covered.

Slight display and calling before flying off, after a stay until it is mate

11 Pair of little terns, *Sterna albifrons*, Lligwy Bay, June 3rd, 1942.

12 Oystercatchers, *Haematopus ostralegus,* on the rocks near Traeth Bychan, April 28th, 1946.

Two Great Black-backs swimming
at the edge of the weed. One holding
wings outside flank feathers.

13 Pair of great black-backed gulls, *Larus marinus*, 1944 or 1945.

May 19th Malltraeth
Lake.

Little Terns feeding from
lake and would rest in
groups on the mud in company
with Dunlin and Common
Terns.

14

14 Little terns, *Sterna albifrons*, feeding and resting, Malltraeth Lake, May 19th, 1945.

31

15 Autumn sandwich terns, *Sterna sandvicensis*, and one common tern, Lligwy Bay, September 8th, 1944.

Sept 10. Nant Bychan Rocks. Evening.
Oystercatchers, Ring Plover and a Teal
The rising tide caused the birds to
take fresh positions periodically. Once
the Teal was awash but maintained
its footing on the weed covered rock. Later
it flew onto the sea and looked very pretty riding the
[signature] .44.

16 Oystercatchers, *Haematopus ostralegus*, ringed plover, *Charadrius hiaticula*, and a teal, *Anas crecca*, Nant Bychan rocks, evening, September 10th, 1944.

Inside of legs dusky yellow ochre

Oct 2ⁿᵈ. Probably Juvenile Guillemot changing to 1ˢᵗ winter.

17 Juvenile guillemot, *Uria aalge*, changing to first winter plumage, October 2nd, 1948.

18 Razorbill, *Alca torda*, in winter plumage, probably autumn 1947.
19 Guillemots, *Uria aalge*, Handa Island, Sutherland, June 16th, 1939.

Guillemott.   Handa Island June 16.
3 sitting together in a sheltered locker of rock exposed
to the sun. Much neck stretching and peering as I drew
them

Leaden   Sepia Brown   Black

20 Common tern, *Sterna hirundo,* on rocks above Porth Aber, June 1942.

Common Tern.

Amlwch

One bringing fish and presenting it to another; this is accompanied by much calling and posturing.

21 Common terns, *Sterna hirundo*, one presenting a fish, Amlwch, June 1942.

June 2nd Amlwch Rocks
(Opposite Amlwch Island on which were
many Terns)
Common Terns. Facing a high wind. They often
spread their tails to preserve balance.

On the shelves of Amlwch Island they squatted close and looked like a mass of
food-grey eggs.

22 Common terns, *Sterna hirundo,* facing a high wind, Amlwch, June 2nd, 1942.
23 Studies of guillemots, *Uria aalge,* Stack Rock, June 12th, 1938.

Black-heads. Traeth Bychan. Sept 4th.
One with a very pronounced rosy breast and
undersides. Others with less noticeable rosy tinge

Traces of the black-brown
hood still to be seen in
this bird.

From memory

24

24 Autumn black-headed gulls, *Larus ridibundus*, and an immature herring gull, *Larus argentatus*,
Traeth Bychan, September 4th, 1944.
25 Black-headed gulls, *Larus ridibundus*, swimming, Iona, September 19th, 1934.

"Black Headed Gull.
Sept. 19ᵗʰ IONA.

June 5ᵗʰ Nant Bychan
            Rock

Turnstones. Small flock of 8 or 9.
One very fine cock bird among them.
Plumage of the others very varied
me confusing.

26 Turnstones, *Arenaria interpres,* at Nant Bychan rocks, June 5th, 1942.

27 Little tern, *Sterna albifrons*, in evening sunlight, Traeth Bychan, June 3rd, 1942.

Nant Bychan Rocks.
Small party of Turnstones hunted these rocks
during our stay. among them one very fine adult ♂ bird

28

28 Turnstones, *Arenaria interpres,* at Nant Bychan rocks, June 1942.

Resting pose   Interrupting Preening to watch me.   Resting

June. 4th 42
Nant Bychan Rocks

This group not actually
seen but the various
poses noted in individual
birds as they rested simply on
the rocks

29 Oystercatchers, *Haematopus ostralegus*, at Nant Bychan rocks, June 4th, 1942.

30 Black-headed gulls, *Larus ridibundus*, showing variation in first summer plumage, Malltraeth Lake, June 2nd, 1944.

Waders

31 Wood sandpiper, *Tringa glareola*, probably a juvenile, Cob Lake, August 20th, 1952.

august 20th. Ash Lake.
Wood Sandpiper. Probably a juvenile

also seen up to Oct 15ᵗʰ on the shore

Oct. 5! Grey Plover. on shore in front of the house. 1 in the morning
feeding on worms   4 in the evening

32

32 Grey plover, *Pluvialis squatarola*, on the shore at Malltraeth, October 5th, 1950.

Curlew Sandpiper. Malltraeth Lake
first week in September. Usually with
Dunlin but occasionally in a flock
exclusively of C. Sandpers.

33 Curlew sandpiper, *Calidris ferruginea*, Malltraeth Lake, September 1945.
34 Knot, *Calidris canutus*, feeding at Cob Lake, September 12th, 1952.
35 The same three knot, four days later.

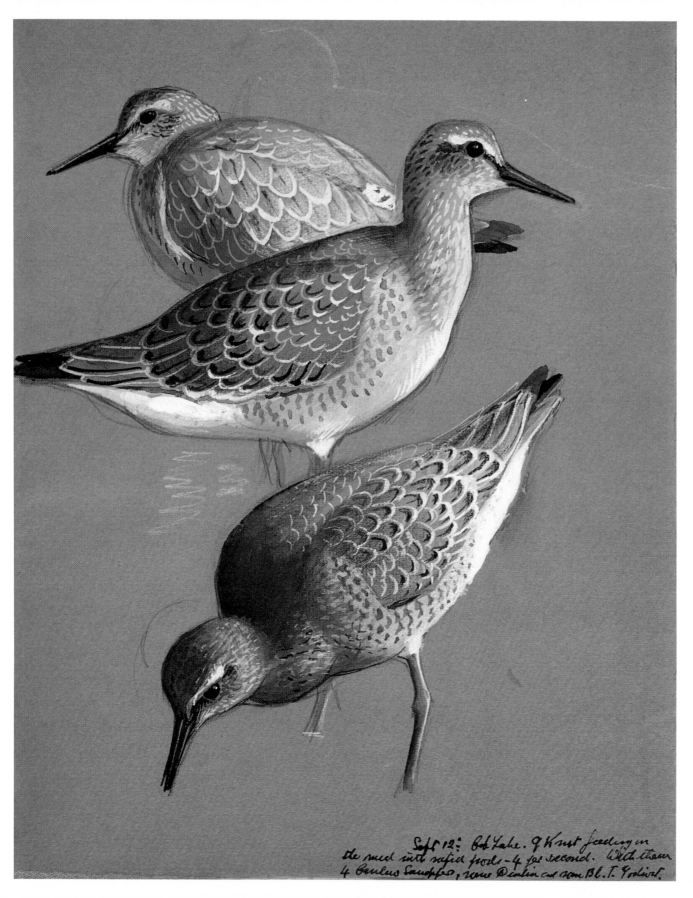

Sept 12: Bob Lake. 9 Knot feeding in
the mud into rapid pools - 4 per second. With them
4 Curlew Sandpiper, now @ calm and some Bl. T. Godwit.

34

Sept. 16ᵗ. 3 Knots on Loch Lake still.
Also 1 Bar T. Godwit 6 B/T. Godwit. Many Dunlin.
3 Little Stints. 1 Greenshank. Herons Swans Gulls.
(black headed) 1 Oyster catcher, Cormorant.

35

Aug 2nd. Young Lapwing. N.B. Under tail coverts casting up above tail.

36 Studies of juvenile lapwing, *Vanellus vanellus*, August 2nd, 1948.

In some birds this pale margin to the mantle very noticeable.

May 18ᵗ Dunlin on the mud of Cob Lake.

37

37 Dunlin, *Calidris alpina,* in breeding plumage at Cob Lake, May 18th, 1949.

38

38 Solitary ruff, *Philomachus pugnax,* at Malltraeth Lake, September 9th, 1946.

39 Sanderlings, *Calidris alba*, at the tide edge, Lligwy Beach, September 8th, 1948.

40 Adult ruff, *Philomachus pugnax*, in moult. Two views of the same bird, Cob Lake, August 26th, 1952.

41 Curlew sandpipers, *Calidris ferruginea*, with a dunlin, *Calidris alpina*, (right centre) Cob Lake, September 9th, 1952.

Och Labe. Aug 26'
Adult Ruff in moult.
Doing much preening

(Two views of the same
bird)

40

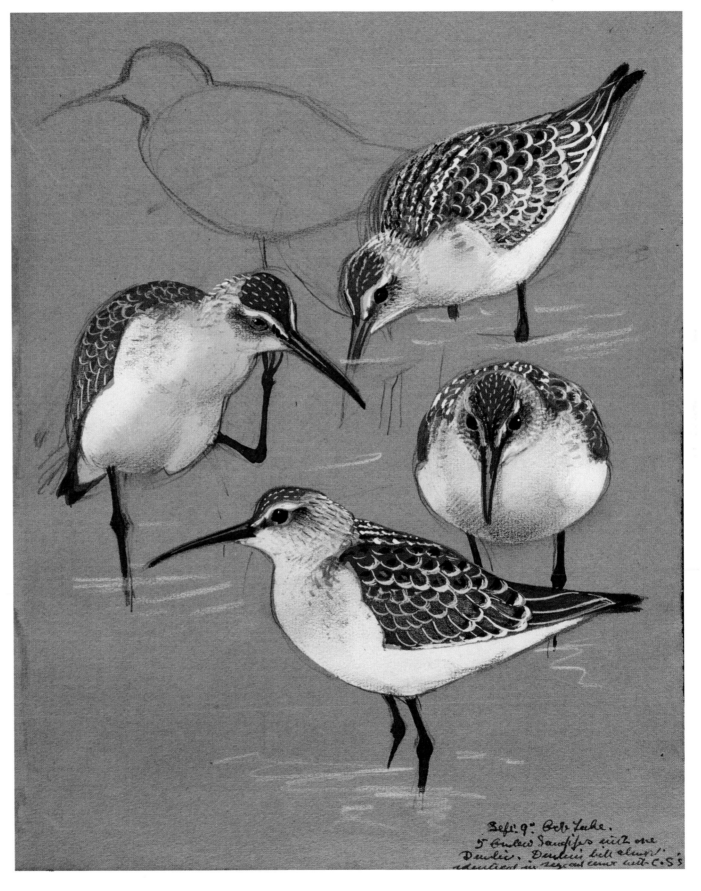

Sept 9. Belt Lake.
5 Curlew Sandpiper with one
Dunlin. Dunlin's bill almost
identical in length and with C.S's

Ruffs. Sept 2nd to Sept 10th

Malltraeth field pools. 5 has the greatest
number seen. Variation in size very apparent
the larger birds appearing more suffused with
warm buff. the smaller more black & white in
the lacing of the scapulars & wings

Will often stand more
erect than this

42

42 Ruffs, *Philomachus pugnax*, at Malltraeth Field pools, September 2nd to 10th, 1945.

43 Black-tailed godwit, *Limosa limosa*, feeding, Glan Avon, September 1944.

Stroking its bill and its middle claw.

May 4. Foll Ferry. Heron perches on side-rail of the ferry causeway.

This white tip not always present in immr. birds seen today

May 4th. Mrs Wright Marsh. Hangatto. Immature Lesser Black Backs. Several feeding on pasture in company with adult L.B.Bs and Herring Gulls.

Redshank (First Winter Plumage)
Malltraeth Lake Sept. 15

44 Heron, *Ardea cinerea*, at Foel Ferry and immature lesser black-backed gull, *Larus fuscus*, at Malltraeth, May 4th, 1952.

45 Redshank, *Tringa totanus*, Malltraeth Lake, September 15th, 1946.

May 3rd & 4th.
Small flock of Dunlin on Bob Lake. All birds in bright new plumage, very fresh and clean. A migrating flock. Feeding belly deep by the shore.

May 3rd & 4th. Common Sandpipers on shores of Bob Lake. 3 birds. One of the birds was browner in colour than other two and its eye stripe was pale buff whereas on the others it was white

46 Dunlin, *Calidris alpina*, in breeding plumage and common sandpipers, *Tringa hypoleucos*,
Cob Lake, May 3rd and 4th, 1952.

47 Black-tailed godwits, *Limosa limosa*, and a snipe, *Gallinago gallinago*, Field Pools, Bont Farm,
early August, 1948.

48

48 Greenshank, *Tringa nebularia*, at Cob Lake. Wind ruffling feathers. March 27th, 1952.
49 Little stints, *Calidris minuta*, at Cob Lake, September 12th and 13th, 1952.

Little Stints. Bob Lake. Sept. 12-13.

Either a pair or a single bird seen at intervals
for some days. When feeding with Dunlin etc. did
rise with the flock but
keep on the margin
of it.

feather shaking

On Sept. 16 this later bird
appeared with two others.

50

50 Studies of purple sandpipers, *Calidris maritima*, at Llandwyn Lighthouse, January 8th, 1950.
51 Bar-tailed godwits, *Limosa lapponica*, at Iona, September 24th, 1934.

Sept. 24ᵗʰ IONA.   Godwit.   On tide edge feeding with Oyster catches.
In small numbers 5 or 6

In size slightly less than Oyster catches
which disthave seem from their feeding.

52

52 Pair of curlew, *Numenius arquata*, feeding on rough pasture, Goldsitch Moss, April 14th, 1947.

53 Studies of young spoonbill, *Platalea leucorodia*, Foryd estuary, October 15th, 1950.

after swallowing fish its passage could be observed down the neck of the heron

Straining to Swallow the fish.

Trying to disgorge it.

Nov 14ᵗʰ. By Shorelands. Heron with flat-fish stuck in its throat. In this state for perhaps ½ hour. Could neither swallow it nor vomit it for a time.

Picking it up again after disgorging it.

54

54 Immature heron, *Ardea cinerea*, swallowing a flatfish, Shorelands, November 14th, 1947.

Dark grey centres
Pale edges

Dark streaked

Dark grey
Pale fawn

Aug 31st. Malltraeth Pool.
Curlew Sandpiper. 3 with a flock
of 20 Dunlin feeding on the mud
of the shallows there in company with
Black tailed Godwit.

55 Curlew sandpiper, *Calidris ferruginea*, at Malltraeth Pool, August 31st, 1945.

May 12th London Zoo
Bird in foreground with less contrast of black
and white especially on back and inner secondaries
(more poses in rough note-book)

56

56 Avocets, *Recurvirostra avosetta*, at London Zoo, May 12th, 1949.
57 Lapwings, *Vanellus vanellus*, at Redesmere, March 12th, 1939.

Lapwing. Rydemere. March 12th

This bird had a black chin and throat but still had pale edges to the hinder scapulars.

Feeding on pasture and between its finds kept patting the ground with its foot. The leg trembled as it was raised and brought down on the flat of the foot.

This bird had a very mottled throat and chin and the black on the chest was also broken as above. Buffish face and pale edges to the hinder scapulars.

58

58 Black-tailed godwits, *Limosa limosa*, Malltraeth Field Pool, August 2nd, 1948.

Geese, Ducks and Swans

82 Grey lags grazing in a marshy field. Jan 4th 51

59 Grey lag, *Anser anser*, grazing in a marshy field, January 4th, 1951.

60 Barnacle goslings, *Branta leucopsis*, from sketches made at Kendal, July 27th, 1944.

61 Pair of gadwall, *Anas strepera*, Cemlyn Lake, March 15th, 1951.

Oct. 29th Redesmere. Part of a flock of
32 Canadas resting in the shallows of the
mere. They were not afloat but were standing
on the bottom. Water silvery grey with
subtle darker grey ripples causing the reflections
of geese are tint to become elongated.
Geese were exquisite against the grey background.
Lightest part was the top of the breast which became
a shade of lilac grey below are at the side becoming
pale grey-brown darkening to sepia at the end of flanks.
Backs were a soft brown the pale edges of feathers not
apparent unless one looked for them.

one goose had
a peculiar dinner of
sepia faun down at
the back of the upper neck

62

62 Canada geese, *Branta canadensis*, at Redesmere, October 29th, 1944.
63 Grey lag, *Anser anser*, in wing moult, Y Felin, July 12th, 1952.

Feb 24th Malltraeth Lake.
Variation of colour on the bills of
Bewick's Swans.

64 Studies of bill markings in Bewick's swans, *Cygnus columbianus*, Malltraeth Lake,
February 24th, 1946.

65 Domestic goose, *Anser domesticus*, August 1942.

66 Flying great crested grebe, *Podiceps cristatus*, and (below) coot chick, *Fulica atra*, Redesmere,
June 9th, 1938.

June 9th
Redsnove.

Grebe (Acclit) flying.
Legs and feet very conspicuous
trailing behind. Wing beats rapid.

About to land.

Bluish scarlet

P. scarlet

Ginger down on a amber base.

Pale down

Young Coot.
June 9th
Redesmere.

Where the light is
behind the bird the
beak looks semi-
transparent and the
tip dark (probably
denser at the tip)
but when the light
is on the beak the tip
is pale.

A brood of 4 being fed by
the parent birds on what looked
like young tender, pale lily shoots.

66

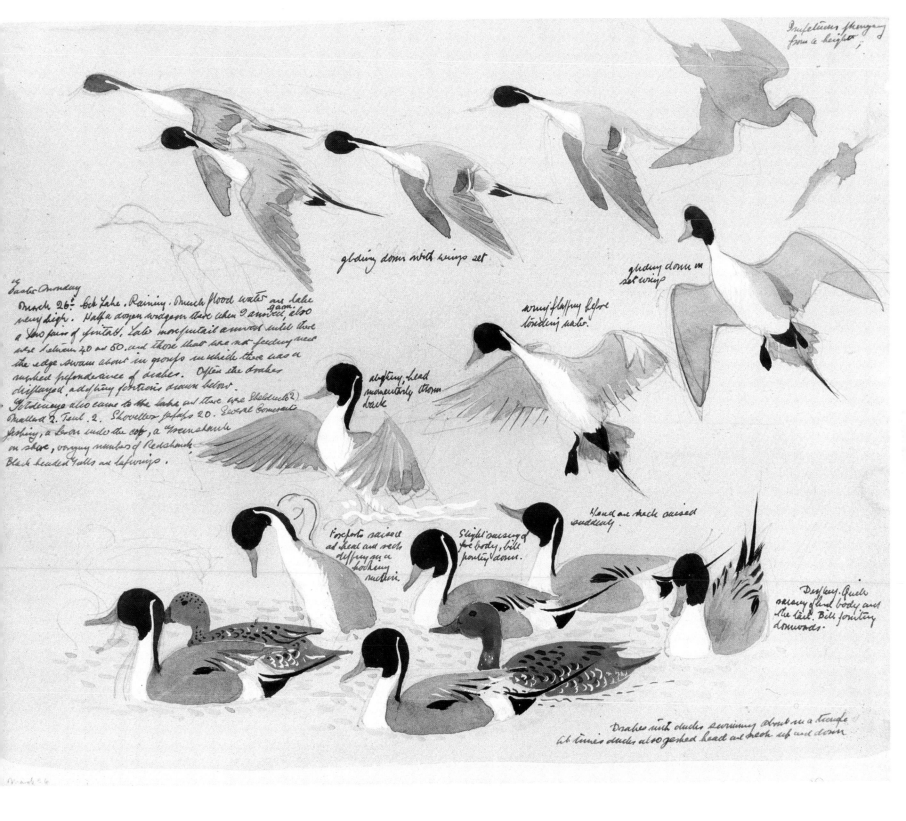

67 Pintails, *Anas acuta*, at Cob Lake, Easter Monday, March 26th, 1951.

First position when alarmed →

2nd position ↓

Younger Geese have not nearly such a large Knob and no orange showing ←

Chinese Geese.   Nov. 24

Bradley Hall
Mr Clitheroe

68

Red breasted Geese. Zoo. May 22nd.

68 Domestic Chinese goose, *Anser cygnoides*, Bradley Hall, near Clitheroe, November 24th, 1934.

69 Red-breasted geese, *Branta ruficollis*, at London Zoo, May 22nd, 1952.

70 Studies of Bewick's swans, *Cygnus columbianus*, taking off and landing, Malltraeth Lake, February 1946.

71 Domestic goose, *Anser domesticus*, August 1942.

Wing stretching.

Sometimes the wing is brought back so that
its inner secondaries are covering tail, rump
and part of the other wing. This side wing is
usually held a little apart from the body whilst
in the stretching position but is not in any way opened

The two cobs approaching each other necks back wings dropped and plumes raised. Usually unturned walk.

the first flurry, each tries to fasten onto the neck of the other. One succeeds and attempts to press the other to the ice

Loosing his grip on neck he loops his own neck over back of opponent and presses down. Eventually he manages to grip his opponents neck, gets on top of him and presses down until his opponents neck and head are flat on ice

...ates they break away and the chase and the struggles goes ...from place to place on the ice. At times they run over the ...ce at others they are just air-borne and when coming onto ...ice they skid for yards before coming to a standstill.

Often on coming to rest the birds seemed too exhausted to stand up. At intervals the rest of the families approached the fighting birds but did not take part in the fighting.

Redesmere. Jan 21st 46

Landing on ice they skid along on their feet and tails

72 Further studies of the domestic goose, including wing-stretching, August 1942.
73 Male swans, *Cygnus olor*, fighting, Redesmere, January 21st, 1946.

Iris. Grey with tinge of amber.

Pale yellowish buff

Sepia with a tinge of auburn or chestnut

Warmer sepia here

Dark sepia

Penduline ridge down centre of bill

Cobalt
Pale dull blue ground with darker slate grey marks.

Nail puce verging to red

Pale cream or yellow.

Slate black

In one duckling this dark mark extended down the whole of the hind neck

'Great' variation in colour of down. One duckling had no dark sepia but was pale yellow all over except for a darker brown crown and nape and stripe behind eye.

Slate

Claws pale horvid

Pale yellowish flesh

Amount of slate black on legs varies considerably. Sometimes toes are quite devoid of black.

Northwich.
June 30º. Muscovy ducklings —

74 Muscovy ducklings, *Cairina moschata*, Northwich, Cheshire, June 30th, 1947.
75 Mallard drake, *Anas platyrhynchos*, Serpentine, London and (below) pintail drake, *Anas acuta*, at London Zoo, May 11th, 1938.

New dark feathers here.

Rest of scapulars being faded, almost silvery.

Aug 27th Young Sheld duck on front of 18 on Cob Lake.

76

76 Young shelduck, *Tadorna tadorna*, at Cob Lake, August 8th, 1951.

TY GWYN. May 26th   Shelduck on the Green Marsh.

...nauch on the marsh in pairs. Often one of the pair would be feeding in the shallow ...s while the other would stand by as if on guard. There was some display consisting of ...d and neck movement. Head and neck alternately ...ethed vertically and then curved until bill touched ...brust out chest.

Frequently flew short distances about the marsh, the pair keeping close.

77 Shelduck, *Tadorna tadorna*, on the Green Marsh, Ty Gwyn, May 26th, 1945.

78 Composition study of the white domestic goose, August, 1942.

79 Domestic geese, *Anser domesticus*, at Malltraeth Marsh, September 8th, 1944.

Shelduck   Traeth Bach May 28th

Duck much duller in colour than drake
This male had a very small knob on bill

SHELDUCK

LADIE FOWLS. (Welsh)

80 Shelduck, *Tadorna tadorna* (female in foreground), Traeth Bach, May 28th, 1945.

81 Mallard, *Anas platyrhynchos*, at Redesmere, February 9th, 1946.

82 Canada geese, *Branta canadensis*, at Birtles Pool, March 5th, 1946.

Capesthorne Pool, Sept: 8th Very warm afternoon.
Geese sleepy and rested with heads back.
Bright sunlight. Geese in reflection of yellow, brown
and green reeds. Slight ripple on the water. Fresh
green of lily-leaves (yellow lily) Some reared out of
the water. Geese very sepia in colour.

83 Canada geese, *Branta canadensis*, resting at Capesthorne Pool, September 8th, 1942.
84 Studies of the great crested grebe, *Podiceps cristatus*, and young, Redesmere, July 1935.
85 Drake mallard, *Anas platyrhynchos*, sequence of moult, Gawsworth Pool, July/August 1935.

84

Mallard Drake in Yarnworth eclipse P. July 1st. Pool.

Both these stages seen on the same day.

July 1st

Later stage of moult

Fairly early stage of moult

July 1st
(1)

(2)

Had the beginnings of the white ring on neck as a thin line round the front of the neck. (not seen in this posit.

Aug 18th.

(3)   Aug 4th

Lower Breast of this bird a paly grey with indefinite pinky brown, crescent markings on the outer sides.
(4)   Aug 4th

any 8ᵗ Cob Lake. Juvenile Shelduck strong on
the wing, and without accompanying parents

86 Juvenile shelduck, *Tadorna tadorna*, at Cob Lake, August 27th, 1949.

87 Family of Bewick's swans, *Cygnus columbianus*, Malltraeth Lake, February 20th, 1946.

Barnacle Family at Mrs Abbott's, Sawmill Lane, Kendal.
From drawings made July 27th.
Goslings Hatched July 14th. nest made on the edge of a quarry cliff. Parent birds are birds which were brought by Mrs Abbott on wild-fowling expeditions.

88 Barnacle geese, *Branta leucopsis*, and goslings, Kendal, July 1944.

Feb 15th. Llyn Coron.

Water swarming with duck, chiefly Wigeon, with Shoveller Teal, Tufted, Pochard. Big majority Widgeon the drakes whistling so that the place was full of their calls. One excited group of one duck and five drakes sped us the water this way and that and when the duck came down to the surface other drakes joined the group and at one time she was chased by eight or nine drakes.

Sometimes the duck would suddenly change direction and seemed to cut through the group of pursuing drakes.

Sweeping up in a glide

attitude when swimming about calling. The drake seemed to display a larger patch of white than normal

occasionally this attitude was adopted by a drake when the company alighted

89 Wigeon, *Anas penelope*, at Llyn Coron, February 15th, 1951.

July 6th Redesmere.

Moorhen with young among water lilies. She with wings much crossed and held high. Fed the young with bits from the flowers and also from hiding things from the leaves.

90 Moorhen, *Gallinula chloropus*, with chick, Redesmere, July 6th, 1945.

Birds of Prey

Aug 13ᵗʰ. Shorelands.
Juvenile Little Owl.
Brought in a paper bag
by two boys from Easel Manor.
Could not fly when it came to
us. Fed on rabbit and dead
birds. Aug 15ᵗʰ strong on the
wing and very fit.

Pose adopted when ready to fly off perch.
Often with a bobbing up and down of head and neck.

91 Studies of a juvenile little owl, *Athene noctua,* hand-reared by the artist, Shorelands, August 13th, 1951.

Light was so bad could
not see if there were any
bars or spots on mantle.
Feb 4th. Later irises showed
that mantle was devoid
of markings as was the
hind crown and nape.

Hissing when I
approached close to the cage
On a previous occasion it was
housed in a cage next to that
of some lion cubs and whenever
a cub approached the partition
between the two Snowy hissed
fiercely

92 Snowy owl, *Nyctea scandiaca*, at Chester Zoo, January 29th–February 9th, 1946.

93 Snowy owl, *Nyctea scandiaca*, at Chester Zoo, possibly a young male, January 29th, 1946.

94 Gyr falcon, *Falco rusticolus*, owned by Ronald Stevens, August 1951.

95 Female sparrowhawk, *Accipiter nisus*, on the garden wall, Shorelands, September 1st, 1949.

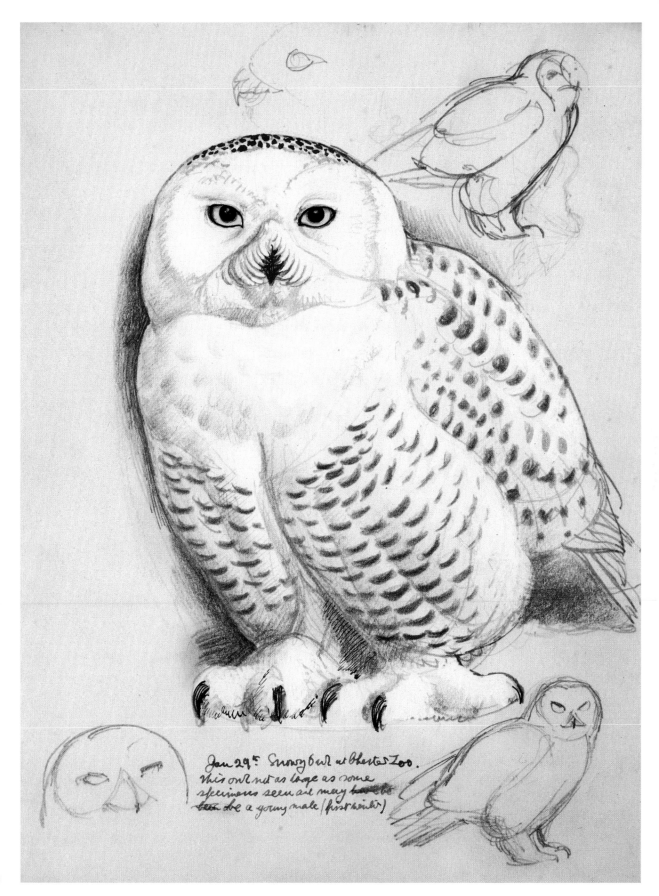

Jan 29ᵗ Snowy Owl at Chester Zoo.
this owl not as large as some
specimens seen and may have
been be a young male (first winter)

93

4 yr Falcon onnedly Ronald Stevens Mid Inyarr.

Sept 1st Evening
Sparrow Hawk on the
garden wall. Rested
for some minutes on the wall
near the kitchen door. No
other birds to be seen.
N.B. Flights are held at the
sides of the tail not
above it.

96

96 Peregrine falcon, *Falco peregrinus*, South Stack, Holy Island, July, probably 1948.

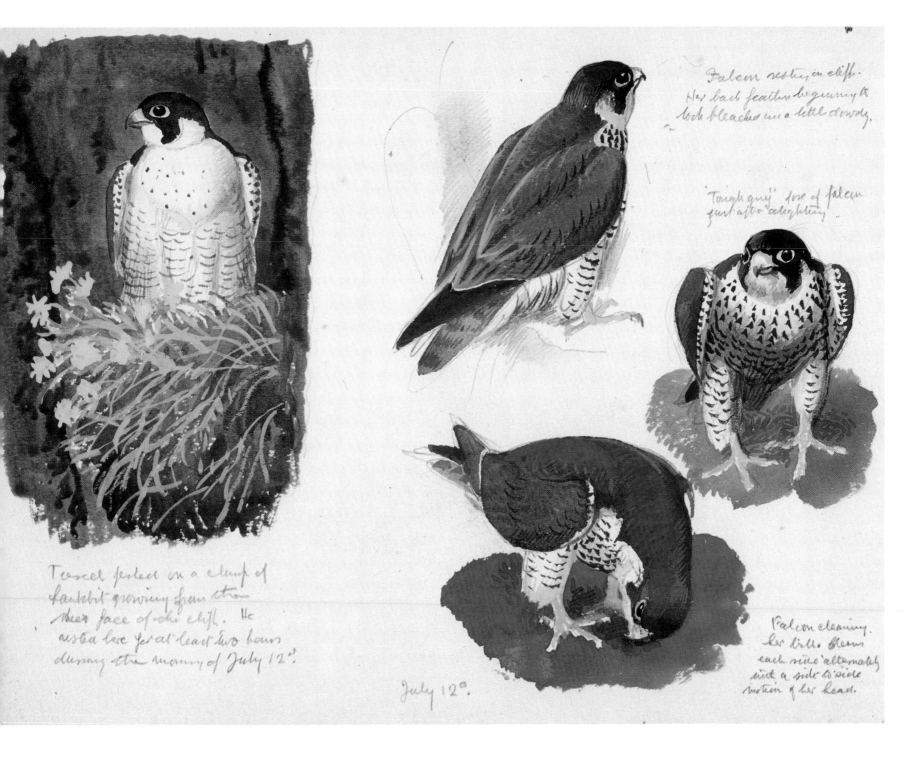

Falcon resting on cliff.
Her back feathers beginning to
look bleached and a little dowdy.

"Tough guy" pose of falcon
just after alighting.

Tiercel perched on a clump of
Sea-kbit growing from the
sheer face of the cliff. He
rested here for at least two hours
during the morning of July 12th.

July 12th

Falcon cleaning
her bill. Cleans
each side alternately
with a side to side
motion of her head.

97 Peregrines, *Falco peregrinus*, at South Stack; the tiercel (left) and falcon, July, probably 1948.

June 30th
Falcon feeding eya
One much more advan
in fledgeing than the
other

98

98 Female ('falcon') peregrine, *Falco peregrinus*, with eyasses, South Stack. June 30th, probably 1948.
99 Study of Ken Williams' Turumti (red-headed) falcon, *Falco chiquera, c.* 1962.
100 & 101 Young sparrowhawks, *Accipiter nisus*, at Hawks-head Clough, July 15th, 1947.
102 Study of a barn owl, *Tyto alba*, autumn 1934.

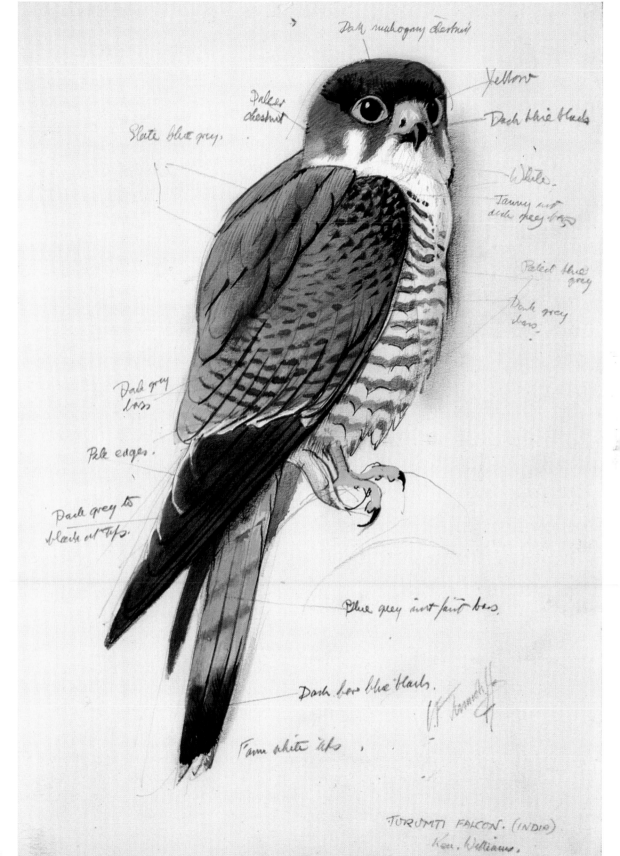

Dark mahogany chestnut

Yellow

Dark blue black

Paler chestnut

Slate blue grey.

White.

Tawny not dark grey bars

Palest blue grey

Dark grey bars.

Dark grey bars

Pale edges.

Dark grey to black at tips.

Blue grey not faint bars.

Dark blue black bars.

Faint white tips.

TURUMTI FALCON. (INDIA)

Ken. Williams.

99

Impression from
memory of the cock
bird which alighted
on nest for an
instant.

Under tail a
silver grey sett
less conspicuous
dark bars.

July 15th Hawks-head Clough

July 15.

Miscellaneous Birds

103 Group of adult and immature ringed plovers, *Charadrius hiaticula*, with turnstones,
Arenaria interpres, behind, Dinas Point, September 7th, 1944.

April 1st Wheatears on stone wall Shorelands
Two perched on the wall and haunted
the vicinity all afternoon.
Both males.
3 days ago saw my first Wheatear
at St Aich by the Lighthouse steps.

April 3rd Hedge near
Crochen Caffo. Two wrens, one
displaying near the other.
Wing vibrating and tail raised
and fanned out while the bird
sang loudly. Sometimes the
wings were raised above the body,
at others held loose as displaying.

104 An early wheatear, *Oenanthe oenanthe*, at Shorelands, and wrens, *Troglodytes troglodytes*, at Crochan Caffo, April, 1951.

105 Singing wren, *Troglodytes troglodytes*, wren collecting nesting material and (below) wood warbler, *Phylloscopus sibilatrix*, and willow warbler, *Phylloscopus trochilus*, May 13th, 1947.

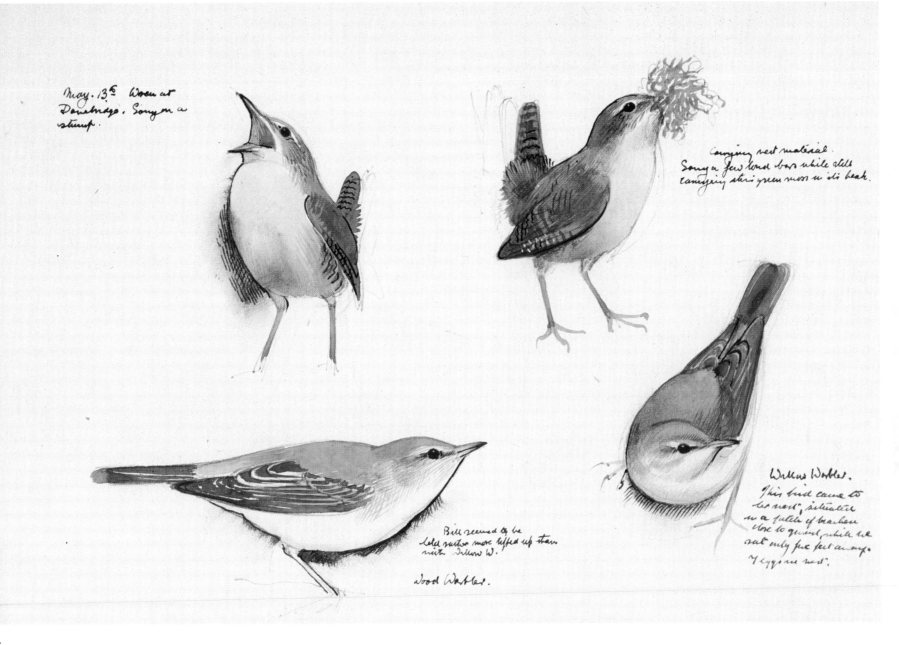

May. 13ᵗ Wren at
Dovebridge. Song on a
stump.

carrying nest material.
Sang a few loud bars while still
carrying string green moss in its beak.

Willow Warbler.
This bird came to
her nest, situated
in a patch of bracken
close to ground, while her
nest only five feet away.
Veggow nest.

Bill seemed to be
held rather more lifted up than
with Willow W.

Wood Warbler.

106 A cock green woodpecker, *Picus viridis*, with two juveniles at Shorelands, July 25th, 1951.
107 Female great spotted woodpecker, *Dendrocopos major*, Chester Zoo, August 3rd, 1939.
108 Young jay, *Garrulus glandarius*, study from a dead bird, July 6th and 7th, 1934.
109 Notes from a day at South Stack, March 10th, 1952.

Shorelands. July 25th.

An adult corn and
two young Green Woodpeckers perched on the shal wall, 8 ± 9 am.
Later all flew down to concrete paving and began to feed
in the craks between the flat stones.
adult called intermittantly as if to keep the young near her.
a high-pitched clear note repeated about 3 times per second.
Call of juveniles rather reedy and throaty, not quite so high as adult.

Under or juvenile
all for dull brown
and in most lights
the eye appears dark

adult wing
stretching

Young Jay. (from dead bird) July 6th ♀.
Blue feathers on the wing not so definately
marked with black & white as in adult bird.
Also head neck and back browner
Length when stretched out about 12".

I

March 10ᵗʰ Soth Stack. From the lighthouse steps, and looking through the hole in the rock, saw two Fulmars resting on the ledges and also saw another flying about the cliffs. Near them a group of Guillemots (8) also rested on the ledges and in the same vicinity a few groups of 2 and 3 Guillemots. While we watched they all left the cliff as if alarmed at our scrutiny. Razorbills were seen flying about the cliffs and over the water but none rested on the cliffs.

Later a Peregrine calling flew out from the cliff beyond Helen's Tower and as we climbed the steps a pair of Ravens flew about the cliffs. In a triangular niche in the cliff was a pile of nest material and I thought I detected new material in the cup (this the site of a previous Raven's nest)

All the previous year's guano had been washed from the cliffs.

There were about 30 Guillemots on the ledges when we arrived.

Herring Gulls were dotted about the cliffs in pairs as if they had already staked out their claims for nesting sites

Later we climbed the steps and went down the headland by Helen's Tower. On the way down watched a cock Stonechat singing on a rock. As he sang he moved his tail up and down, and his throat throbbed as he sang. Gorse was coming into flower, some of it well out though in its seaward side it was very brown as if it had been burnt — the results of salt-laden gales I suppose. Looking from the cliff edge down to the sea we saw a solitary Shag swimming. In previous years a solitary pair had nested near the foot of these cliffs

Moving along the cliff path a Peregrine again went out from the cliff calling hoarsely. It flew about and glided for a time then turned up the headland and disappeared over the skyline.

Near the place where the great cliffs jut out almost at right angles to the general line a pair of Ravens left the cliff and flew about suspiciously, but here we could find no sign of a nest. Later they returned and flew round again, but we still failed to find a nest or nest of one.

When we returned to Helen's Tower a Peregrine flew out from its cliff opposite, again calling, and after circling very over the sea and the lighthouse came into the cliff again but this time rested out of sight in the cliff opposite the steps. While in flight it was several times mobbed by herring gulls but easily eluded them.

109

110 Goldfinch, *Carduelis carduelis*, feeding young at Shorelands, September 19th, 1949.

Mid aft.
Oct 15ᵗʰ '51 Hoopoe.
First seen flying
up from the drive. It
flew to the shore and
settled to feed on the
little saltings, thrusting
its bill vertically down.
Then it flew to a stone
and rested for a time before
flying off over the bungalow

Resting on a stone.

Feeding.

Alert and ready to fly.

III Hoopoe, *Upupa epops,* at Shorelands, October 1951.

Aug. 14th Clough Brook, Wildboarclough.
Cock Grey Wagtail in moult.
Outer tail feathers half-grown.
Remains of black throat still visible
Some inner secondaries missing.

When preening, dropped wings
so that lower back and rump
was visible.

112

112 Cock grey wagtail, *Motacilla cinerea*, in moult, Clough Brook, August 14th, 1944.
113 Juvenile long-tailed tit, *Aegithalos caudatus*, Radnor Mere, June 26th, 1939.

Looks very
plump when at ease

Wheatears on the dried-up bed of
Bodey Reservoir feeding on worms. April 28th

June 9ᵗʰ Cob Lake Shore.

Feeding

114 Studies of a cock wheatear, *Oenanthe oenanthe*, Bosley Reservoir, April 28th, 1938.
115 A ruff, *Philomachus pugnax*, in breeding plumage, Cob Lake, June 9th, 1949.

116 Cuckoo, *Cuculus canorus*, on barbed wire, April 1946.

March 13th Redesmere.
Small company of Redpolls – 6 or 7 birds.
feeding on the alders at the side of
mere. Sometimes they dropped to the
ground and searched among dead leaves
and plants and grasses.   Day of cold wind

One hen observed has a very
grey bird with very pronounced
light wing bars..

117 Redpolls, *Acanthis flammea*, on an alder branch, Redesmere, March 13th, 1946.

118 Greenfinch, *Carduelis chloris*, feeding young, Alderley Edge, August 22nd, 1944.
119 Spotted flycatcher, *Muscicapa striata*, with young, Gawsworth, July 11th, 1944.

April 6th. Radnor Woods. Gt. Sp. Woodpecker.

120

120 Great spotted woodpecker, *Dendrocopos major*, Radnor Woods, April 6th, 1947.
121 Cock chaffinch, *Fringilla coelebs*, at Redesmere, March 9th, 1939.

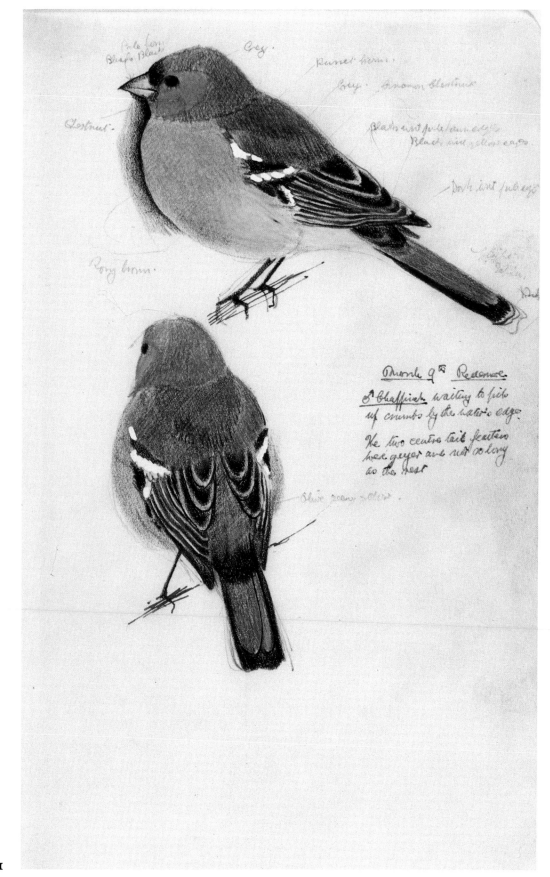

Grey.

Russet brown.

Grey. Cinnamon Chestnut

Black and pale brown edges
Black and yellow edges

Dark tint pale edge

Chestnut.

Pale horn
Black & Black

Rosy brown.

March 9th Redcome.
♂ Chaffinch waiting to pick
up crumbs by the water's edge.

The two centre tail feathers
were greyer and not so long
as the rest

Olive green yellow.

Pont Aber Glaslyn. May 1st. 1952. Two ♂ and one ♀
Pied Flycatcher seen near the bridge. One male flew
to a hole in an oak, the entrance to last year's nest
of Pied Flycatchers. It is clear that the pair intend
to use this same site. Several times the other male
was chased away by the paired male.

122 Two male pied flycatchers, *Muscicapa hypoleuca*, and a female, Pont Aber Glaslyn, May 1st, 1952.

123 Studies of pied flycatchers, *Muscicapa hypoleuca*, at Pont Aber Glaslyn, April 22nd, 1951.

C. F. Tunnicliffe was born at Langley, Cheshire on 1st December 1901. Shortly afterwards his parents moved to Lane End Farm, Sutton, where he attended the village school and from there obtained a scholarship to Macclesfield Art School. He studied at Manchester Academy of Fine Art before winning a Royal Exhibition Scholarship to the Royal College of Art in 1921. He obtained his diploma for painting in 1923.

He was elected Associate of the Royal Academy of Arts in 1944 and elected R.A. in 1954.

In August 1974 an exhibition of his bird drawings opened at the Royal Academy. In the same year he was awarded the Gold Medal of the Royal Society for the Protection of Birds, of which he was a Vice-President. He received the O.B.E. in the Queen's Birthday Honours list of 1977.

He died at Malltraeth, Anglesey in February 1979.